Taylor Lautner
Twilight Star

Maggie Murphy

PowerKiDS press.

New York

Published in 2011 by The Rosen Publishing Group, Inc.
29 East 21st Street, New York, NY 10010

First Edition

Book Design: Greg Tucker
Photo Researcher: Jessica Gerweck

Photo Credits: Cover Steve Granitz/WireImage/Getty Images; pp. 5, 15 Kevin Mazur/WireImage/Getty Images; pp. 7, 19 John Shearer/ WireImage/Getty Images; p. 9 Jeffrey Mayer/WireImage/Getty Images; p. 11 Lester Cohen/WireImage/Getty Images; p. 12–13 Dominique Charriau/WireImage/Getty Images; p. 17 Jon Furniss/WireImage/ Getty Images; p. 21 Eric Charbonneau/WireImage/Getty Images; p. 22 Michael Tran/WireImage/Getty Images.

Library of Congress Cataloging-in-Publication Data

Murphy, Maggie.
  Taylor Lautner : Twilight star / Maggie Murphy. — 1st ed.
      p. cm. — (Young and famous)
  Includes index.
  ISBN 978-1-4488-0642-3 (library binding) —
ISBN 978-1-4488-1797-9 (pbk.) — ISBN 978-1-4488-1798-6 (6-pack)
  1. Lautner, Taylor, 1992—Juvenile literature. 2. Actors—United States—Biography—Juvenile literature. I. Title.
  PN2287.L2855M87 2011
  791.4302'8092—dc22
  [B]
                              2009050881

Manufactured in the United States of America

CPSIA Compliance Information: Batch #WS10PK: For Further Information contact Rosen Publishing, New York, New York at 1-800-237-9932

Contents

Meet Taylor Lautner   4

Twilight **Star**   8

A Great Actor   16

Books   23

Web Sites   23

Glossary   24

Index   24

Taylor Lautner is a movie star.

5

Taylor was born in Grand Rapids, Michigan. Now he lives in Los Angeles, California.

Taylor is **famous** for starring in the *Twilight* movies.

9

He plays the **role** of Jacob Black. Jacob can turn into a wolf.

Taylor likes **spending** time with the other *Twilight* actors.

Taylor is friends with other young stars. He knows Miley Cyrus.

Taylor has also acted in other movies. He was in *Valentine's Day*.

Taylor has won **awards** for his acting. He won a 2009 Teen Choice Award.

Taylor's fans think he is a great actor.

Taylor will be a star
for a long time
to come.

Books

Here are more books to read about Taylor Lautner:

Ryals, Lexi. *Taylor Lautner: Breaking Star.* New York: Price Stern Sloan, 2009.

Williams, Mel. *Taylor Lautner: Overnight Sizzlin' Sensation.* New York: Simon Pulse, 2009.

Web Sites

Due to the changing nature of Internet links, PowerKids Press has developed an online list of Web sites related to the subject of this book. This site is updated regularly. Please use this link to access the list:
www.powerkidslinks.com/young/tl/

Glossary

awards (uh-WORDZ) Honors given to people.

famous (FAY-mus) Very well known.

role (ROHL) A part played by a person in a movie, TV show, or play.

spending (SPEND-ing) Passing or using.

Index

A

actor(s), 12, 20

C

Cyrus, Miley, 14

F

fans, 20
friends, 14

G

Grand Rapids, Michigan, 6

L

Los Angeles, California, 6

M

movies, 8, 16

R

role, 10

V

Valentine's Day, 16